MOVE AND GET HEALTHY!

LET'S MOVE IN THE OUTDOORS

WRITTEN BY
JACKIE HERON

ILLUSTRATED BY
TATEVIK AYAKYAN

magic wagon

Content Consultant:
Jonathan Martin
Physical Education Teacher, Nova Classical Academy

VISIT US AT WWW.ABDOPUBLISHING.COM

Published by Magic Wagon, a division of the ABDO Group, PO Box 398166, Minneapolis, MN 55439. Copyright © 2012 by Abdo Consulting Group, Inc. International copyrights reserved in all countries. All rights reserved. No part of this book may be reproduced in any form without written permission from the publisher.

Looking Glass Library™ is a trademark and logo of Magic Wagon.

Printed in the United States of America, North Mankato, Minnesota.
102011
012012

 THIS BOOK CONTAINS AT LEAST 10% RECYCLED MATERIALS.

Text by Jackie Heron
Illustrations by Tatevik Avakyan
Edited by Melissa York
Design and production by Emily Love

Library of Congress Cataloging-in-Publication Data

Heron, Jackie.
  Let's move in the outdoors / by Jackie Heron ; illustrated by Tatevik Avakyan.
    p. cm. — (Move and get healthy!)
  Includes index.
  ISBN 978-1-61641-862-5
  1. Physical fitness for children—Juvenile literature. I. Avakyan, Tatevik, 1983- ill. II. Title.
  GV443.H44 2012
  613.7042—dc23
                            2011033084

TABLE OF CONTENTS

FOR ALL SEASONS

Every season has outdoor activities for you to enjoy. Think about how you feel when you play outside. You connect with nature. Your senses come alive. You have more energy even the next day!

5

When you play outdoors, you make new friends. You see new things and have new, fresh ideas. You become more sure of yourself. You make your muscles stronger and leaner.

Your body needs oxygen to work. When you exercise, you breathe deeper and faster. You take in more oxygen. Your heart beats faster. It sends more oxygen to your muscles. When you exercise more, your body uses oxygen better.

SAFETY FIRST

Follow these tips to keep you safe outdoors:

❊ Know your way to the activity and home again.

❊ Listen to your grown-ups and follow their rules.

❊ Dress for the weather. Is it cold out? Wear plenty of layers. Don't forget your hat, mittens, scarf, and boots!

❊ Wear a life jacket while you're in or near the water.

❊ Wear your helmet and pads when you're biking or skating.

❊ Wear shoes and socks that are made for your activity. You need boots for hiking. You need sneakers for skateboarding.

❊ Drink lots of water. If you're thirsty, you are dehydrated.

Take a backpack with supplies when you spend a day in the woods. Always bring water. Healthy snacks, a compass, a map, and binoculars are useful. Don't forget your first aid kit.

S-T-R-E-T-C-H IT OUT

Remember to stretch before you begin your trek. Stretching warms up your muscles. It makes them more flexible. It can help prevent injuries.

LEG LUNGES

Leg lunges are good stretches. Stand up straight with your legs a little bit apart. Move one foot in front of you about the length of two steps. Lean forward until your knee is in line with your ankle. Touch your other knee lightly to the ground. Step back to your starting position and switch legs.

FOLLOW THE LEADER

Do the squirrel scamper! Lean forward at the waist and put your hands on the ground. Now move your hands and feet as you scamper on all fours like a squirrel.

Feel the muscles in your arms and legs stretching. If your muscles feel tight, practice more stretching.

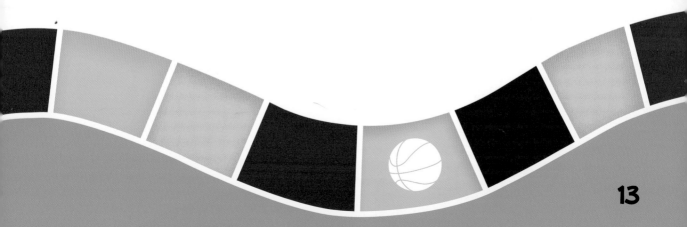

DIGESTION

Your body breaks down the food you eat to make energy. This is called digestion. Playing outdoors helps your body digest food.

❅ When you play outdoors, you get hungrier. Your body wants to eat healthful food.

❅ Your digestive system works better. It turns your food into energy. It will store less food as fat.

❅ Your stomach feels better because it's working. You won't feel slow and stuffed.

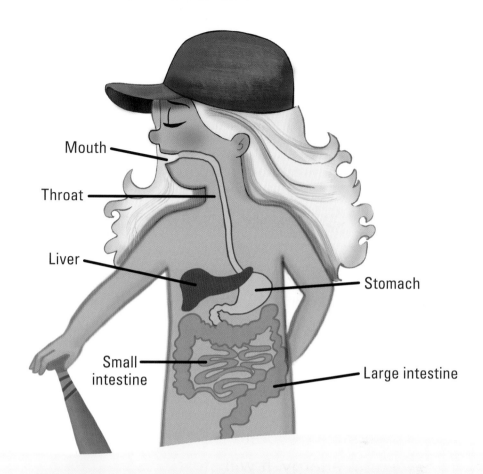

Mouth

Throat

Liver

Small intestine

Stomach

Large intestine

PARTS OF YOUR DIGESTIVE SYSTEM

mouth and throat: take in food when you eat

stomach: breaks down food

liver: makes juices that help break down food

small intestine: separates out waste from the healthy parts that make energy

large intestine: helps waste leave your body

SUNNY SMILES

The right amount of sunlight is good for you.
Your skin will have a healthy shine and feel smooth.
The sun's rays destroy harmful germs that get on
your skin.

WHEN IN THE SUN . . .

※ Wear sunscreen. Don't forget to put it on your ears and nose.
Wear lip protector, too.

※ Protect your eyes with a sun hat or sunglasses.

※ The sun's rays bounce off snow or water. This means you get hit
with more sunlight. Remember to reapply sunscreen or wear long
sleeves to protect yourself.

WINDY MOVES

Run up a hill against a strong wind. Do this again with the wind at your back. Notice the difference? You use more energy when you run against the wind.

On windy days, move against the wind. Fly a kite. Chase around a beach ball. Have a paper airplane race with your friends.

HEALTHY LUNGS

Playing in the wind is healthy. Your lungs are full of tiny air sacs. When you breathe in, fresh air fills the air sacs. This gives your lungs a deep cleaning.

THE BODY'S BEST DEFENSE

Your body has a way to defend you from sickness. It's your immune system. Your immune system is a group of organs, tissues, and cells. It protects you from germs that make you sick.

Playing outside makes your immune system stronger. You grow more of the cells that fight germs. These cells get stronger. It's easier for your body to fight off the germs.

WATCH AND DO

Watch a bird and try to do what it does. Bob your head up and down. Bend at your waist like you're looking for food. Flap your arms and try to fly. A bird's muscles and bones are meant for flying. Yours are for walking and running.

You have most of the same leg bones as a bird. Your thigh is your femur. It is the longest bone in your body. Your lower leg has two bones, the tibia and fibula. However, a bird has no kneecap, or patella.

ARMS AND WINGS

Birds have the same bones in their wings as you do in your arms. They are the humerus, radius, and ulna.

Bird   Human

Femur

Patella

Fibula

Tibia

Ankle

23

CONNECTED TO NATURE

You've learned about the wildlife you've watched. What have you learned about yourself? Did you laugh when you scampered like a squirrel? Was it fun to flap your arms like a bird?

Being out in nature creates special feelings. Do you feel closer to the animals you saw? Put those happy, caring feelings to work helping Earth.

Look around you. What can you do to help Earth? Is there trash to be collected? Can you plant a bird and butterfly garden? Watch grown-ups who help the environment. Talk to a guide at a nature center.

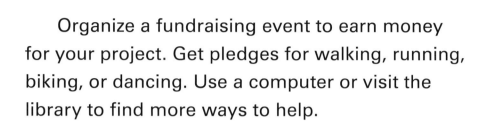

Organize a fundraising event to earn money
for your project. Get pledges for walking, running,
biking, or dancing. Use a computer or visit the
library to find more ways to help.

NEW TRAILS

You can always discover new things outdoors. Here are some fun games to try!

MAKE A MAP

Think of places in your neighborhood. They might be a friend's house, a big tree, or a bus stop. Make a map showing those places. Now draw a route on your map.

Go on a walk with a family member. Can she use your map to follow your route? Have her draw a new map and walk her route.

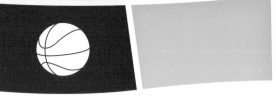

TREASURE HUNT

Make a list of things you might find on a walk. These could be: an interesting rock, a beautiful leaf, a bottle cap, or a piece of sidewalk chalk.

Go on a walk with a friend. Can you find everything on your list?

What three new things can you do outdoors this week?

KEEP MOVING

1. Winter is here. It's cold outside. Did it snow? Shovel snow or build a snow fort. Try skiing or ice skating.

2. It's springtime. Plant, water, and weed some sunflowers. When the flowers are grown, pick the seeds. Ask a grownup to help you dry the seeds. Sunflower seeds are good for you to eat.

3. The sun is shining brightly. It's summertime, and it's hot outside. Splash in a pool or at the beach. Paddle a canoe. Go camping or horseback riding.

4. It's cooler in the autumn. Rake leaves or clean up the garden. Join a new sport, activity, or club at school.

5. Any time of year is a good time for you to walk or run outside. Try the same route in each season. Notice what changes from month to month.

WORDS TO KNOW

binoculars—a device you look through with both eyes to see things that are far away.

compass—a device that shows which way is north.

dehydrated—having lost too much water from your body.

energy—being able to do things without feeling tired.

environment—the air, land, and sea surrounding living things.

flexible—being able to bend or stretch far without feeling pain.

fundraising event—an event that earns money for a cause.

germs—tiny living things that make people sick.

muscle—body tissue, or layers of cells, that help the body move.

oxygen—a colorless gas that humans and animals need to breathe.

pledges—promises to give money.

tissue—a group of cells that forms a body part such as an organ or a muscle.

LEARN MORE

BOOKS

Brunelle, Lynn. *Camp Out!* New York: Workman Publishing Company, 2007.

Carlson, Nancy. *Get Up and Go!* New York: Puffin Books, 2006.

Ward, Jennifer. *Let's Go Outside!* Boston, MA: Trumpeter Books, 2009.

WEB SITES

To learn more about being active outdoors, visit ABDO Group online at **www.abdopublishing.com**. Web sites about being active outdoors are featured on our Book Links page. These links are routinely monitored and updated to provide the most current information available.

INDEX